Crock Pot Slow Cooker Cookbook 2022

Crock Pot Slow Cooker Cookbook 2022

1000-Day Fresh and Delicious Recipes; The Absolute Best Slow Cooker Cookbook, Great Selection of Crock Pot Slow Cooker Recipes for Beginners & Advanced Users

Taylorson Brown

CONTENT

INTRODUCTION

The modern fast paced world we live in makes cooking a difficult task. Days go by incredibly fast with work, time spent in traffic, kids and family and sometimes a proper lunch or dinner is the last of our concerns. But don't you wish you could eat a nutritious meal every day? A Crock Pot slow cooking resolves all your cooking problems regarding time and money.

No matter how busy you get, the Crock Pot slow cooker makes mealtime simple. All you need is a handful of ingredients, a few minutes to prep, and, of course, the Crock Pot Slow Cooker Cookbook 2022.

In this cookbook, you will learn how to cook with the Crock Pot slow cooker like a pro. Each of the meals in this cookbook are health and easy to prepare. You and your family will get the most delicious and the healthiest meals while giving you a bit of a break in the kitchen.

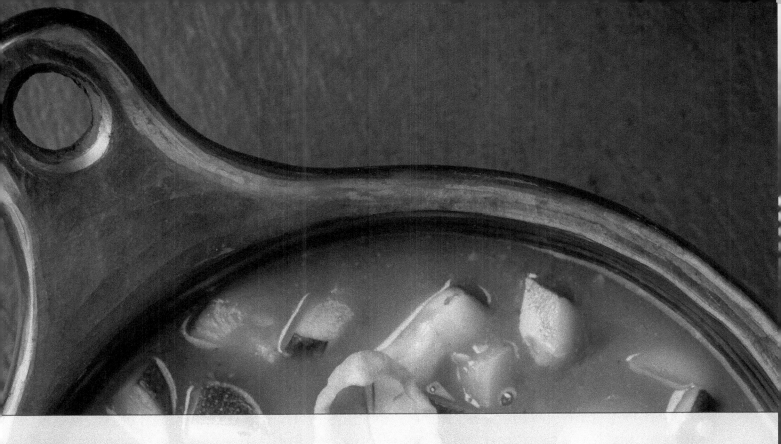

CHAPTER 1: THE BASICS OF CROCK POT SLOW COOKER

As society sees the negative effects that greasy and fast foods have on the human body, Crock Pot slow cooker are more and more popular. Quicker is not always better, as we have seen in a society that is infected with several diseases. If you are one of the thousands that are looking to improve your health, keep meals simple, and enjoy the succulent flavor of foods, this book is just for you.

What is Crock Pot Slow Cooker?

Crock Pot slow cooker is a kitchen appliances that is designed to cook food at extremely low temperatures. This allows the appliances to facilitate hours of unattended cooking while producing an extremely delicious and healthy meal.

Despite common belief though, Crock Pot slow cooker is extremely versatile in nature and you can create almost anything using the Slow Cooker, ranging from roasts, dips, stews, desserts to meats of all kinds! However, it should be noted that slow cooker is considerably safer to use when compared to other Pressure Cookers such, mainly because slow cooker tend to cook on a very low pressure as opposed to the high pressure utilized by pressure cookers.

While the microwave is still a handy tool in everyday living, you will find that your Crock Pot slow cooker has an important place on your kitchen counter.

How to Use Your Crock Pot Slow Cooker

We all love hot delicious meal but we all don't have enough time to prepare it. If you are in a hurry or are a busy person then simply prepare ingredients before going to bed and place ingredients in the refrigerator, and take them out in the morning and start your slow cooker. When you reach home from work, your meal will be ready to serve!

We have been cooking in our slow cooker for years now. Over the course of time, we have picked up some tips and tricks. Slow cookers heat up slowly, usually taking two to three hours to get up to their highest temperature. This ensures that the food retains its nutrients while also preventing scorching or burning. It's also the reason you don't need to be home while the meal cooks. This steam that the slow cooker creates is an important factor in creating those marvelous flavors—foods are cooked in their own steam, literally infusing the flavor back in through the cooking process. This keeps the food moist and works to tenderize the meat and even the most stubborn vegetables.

Learn how almost any type of meal can be created by using your Crock Pot slow cooker. There are many treats that are shown in this book that you never dreamed could be made with a slow cooker. Just keep the following things in mind:

- Cut meat and vegetables to the same size to ensure even cooking in soups and stews.

- Place slow-cooking items such as turnips, potatoes—on the bottom of the slow cooker.

- When cooking traditional slow cooker meals such as soups, stews, and meats, make sure the slow cooker is at least half full. This ensures even cooking.

- Don't thaw food in the slow cooker. Frozen food heats up too slowly to effectively prevent bacterial growth when in a slow cooker. It's better to thaw food overnight in a refrigerator or use the microwave.

Benefits of Crock Pot Slow Cooker

Fresh foods are always the best way to eat, but the convenience of canned and boxed foodstuffs have drawn a fast-paced society away from eating right. The slow cooking is a great way to get back into nutritional eating. There are multiple benefits of Crock Pot slow cooker, a few of these are:

- **Delicious & healthy dishes**

Since preparing in the slow cooker is mainly using fresh ingredients, a low cooking temperature leaves a numerous useful components. Vegetables and meat cooked in the slow cooker give off a lot of juices, soak them up, mix, giving a fuller flavor.

- **Save money**

Slow cookers are great for people cooking on a budget, as the long cooking times are great for the cheaper cuts of meat.

- **Save time**

Slow cooker will save you over-all time by setting it and forget it, the dish will take longer time to cook, however the preparation will be fast.

- **Save energy**

Slow cookers are highly energy efficient, and don't be afraid to leave these on for long periods of time, as they use very little energy when slow cooking.

- **Easy to use**

You don't need to be a cook to be able to chop up some food and throw it into a Crock Pot slow cooking and press a button.

- **Easy clean up**

Slow cooker is the perfect device for one-pot dishes. You can cook your favorite dishes without a lot of dishes for washing.

There are numerous reasons to love Crock Pot slow cooker. Here are just a few of the main advantages, however, the more you'll use this device in the kitchen, this list will increase.

Tips and Suggestions for Crock Pots Slow Cooking

- Use the right size vessel, the cooking process will suffer if you do not load the pot with the proper amount of food/liquid that is required.

- Never open the lid during the cooking process, as this will lose heat that has built up inside, and increasing cooking time.

- Don't spill liquids outside the ceramic insert. If you do spill some by mistake, clean cautiously using a cloth and ensuring that no liquid enters the appliance.

- Reheating food in a slow cooker is not recommended. It will take several hours to reach proper temperatures. Use a microwave instead.

- When using herbs and spices, use half the amount at the beginning of the cooking cycle, and add the rest toward the end. This will help keep the flavors more intense.

- Read your instruction manual carefully. Many glass lids are not dishwasher-safe, although the ceramic container may be.

- Be sure the lid is well-placed over the slow cooker's ceramic insert. It should not be tilted or off center. The steam created during cooking helps create a seal and keeps the heat inside the slow cooker.

- Be familiar to the different tricks so that your food comes out tasting incredible every time.

- Make sure that only fresh ingredients are going into the Crock Pot slow cooker at all times to guarantee that you will not contribute to bacteria growth inside the vessel.

How to Care for Your Crock Pot Slow Cooker

Crock Pot Slow cooker is very easy to clean as compare to the other kitchen appliances. Just wipe the base down inside and out after every use—most of the time all you need is a soft sponge, hot water, and standard dish washing liquid. A little baking soda can be used as a gentle scouring powder to help you scrub off any slightly stuck-on food. Your Crock Pot slow cooker will never get gross and dirty if you clean it properly inside and out after every single use.

Crock Pot Slow cookers are very simple appliances. However, they do need some special care. If you follow these rules your slow cooker will produce healthy meals for many years:

- Never, never, never immerse the slow cooker in water. If it's plugged in at the time, you could receive a shock. If it isn't plugged in, you could damage the heating element.

- Parts of the slow cooker can be cleaned in a dishwasher. If you have a removable crockery core, place it on the bottom rack of the dishwasher. If the crockery container isn't removable, simply use a soft cloth or sponge to wash it out. Always use a damp cloth to wash the metal housing.

- Do not scrub with abrasives, as these can scratch the crock, creating areas for bacteria to reside.

Be sure to follow all of these rules to guarantee your slow cooker will both last for many years and perform at maximum potential with each use.

FAQs

1.Can Crock Pots slow cooker be left unattended?

Yes. One of the main benefits of a slow cooker is that you can put in your ingredients, leave home and come back to a delicious meal.

2.Why meat comes out too dry or too tough?

If your meat is dried out or too tough, there probably was not enough liquid in the recipe or the cooking temperature was too high for that particular cut of meat. While you don't need a lot of liquid for slow cooking, and meat will release its own cooking liquid, you do want to make sure there is some liquid in the slow cooker.

3.Why the food is not cooked evenly?

Certain ingredients in your food may cook faster than others for one of two reasons: Your food was not placed in the slow cooker in the proper order, or pieces of food were not cut to the same size. Make sure your pieces are cut uniformly, as smaller pieces cook faster than larger pieces.

4.How to avoid food burns or sticks to the slow cooker?

There are several reasons your food may burn or stick. The most common reason is that there is not enough liquid. You don't need a lot of liquid, but you do need some—especially for meat dishes.

5.How to clean the slow cooker?

If you have some sticky residue lying in your pot, try making a mixture of baking soda and detergent and sprinkling it over the pot. Let it sit for a while before scrubbing to remove any stuck-on food.

6.How to cook Vegetables with the slow cooker?

Vegetables cook more slowly than meats, in a slow cooker, so put them in first at the bottom and around the sides. Then add meat and cover the food with liquid, such as broth, water, or barbecue sauce.

CHAPTER 2: BREAKFAST

Breakfast Quinoa Pudding

Ingredients:

- 1/4 cup maple syrup
- 3 cups almond milk
- 1 cup quinoa
- 2 tablespoons vanilla extract

Directions:

1. Put quinoa in your slow cooker.
2. Add maple syrup and almond milk and stir.
3. Also add vanilla extract, stir, cover and cook on High for 1 hour and 30 minutes.
4. Stir your pudding again, divide into bowls and serve.
5. Enjoy!

Nutritional Value (Amount per Serving):

- Calories: 140
- Fat: 2
- Carbs: 5
- Protein: 5

Lentils Sandwich

Ingredients:

For the sauce:
- 1/2 cup blackstrap molasses
- 28 ounces canned tomatoes, crushed
- 6 ounces tomato paste
- 1/4 cup white vinegar
- 2 tablespoons apple cider vinegar
- 1 sweet onion, chopped
- 3 garlic cloves, minced
- 1 teaspoon dry mustard
- 1 tablespoon coconut sugar
- 1/4 teaspoon red pepper flakes
- A pinch of sea salt
- 1/4 teaspoon liquid smoke
- A pinch of cayenne
- 4 cups green lentils, cooked and drained

Directions:

1. Put molasses in your slow cooker.
2. Add tomatoes, tomato paste, vinegar, apple cider vinegar, onion, garlic, mustard, sugar, salt, pepper flakes, cayenne and liquid smoke.
3. Stir everything, cover your slow cooker and cook on High for 1 hour and 30 minutes.
4. Add lentils, stir gently, divide on vegan buns and serve for breakfast.
5. Enjoy!

Nutritional Value (Amount per Serving):

- Calories: 150
- Fat: 3
- Carbs: 6
- Protein: 7

Incredible Rice Pudding

Prep Time: 10 Minutes   Cook Time: 3Hours   Serves: 2

Ingredients:

- 1/2 cup coconut sugar
- 2 cups almond milk
- 1/2 cup brown rice
- 1 teaspoon vanilla extract
- 1 tablespoons flax seed meal
- 1/2 cup raisins
- 1 teaspoon cinnamon powder

Directions:

1. Put the milk in your slow cooker.
2. Add rice and sugar and stir well.
3. Also, add flaxseed meal, raisins, vanilla and cinnamon, stir, cover and cook on Low for 2 hours.
4. Stir your pudding again, cover and cook on Low for 1 more hour.
5. Divide into bowls and serve.
6. Enjoy!

Nutritional Value (Amount per Serving):

- Calories: 160
- Fat: 2
- Carbs: 8
- Protein: 12

Tapioca Pudding

Prep Time: 10 Minutes   Cook Time: 2 Hours   Serves: 6

Ingredients:

- 4 cups coconut milk
- 1/2 cup pearl tapioca
- 1 teaspoon vanilla extract
- 2 teaspoons orange extract

Directions:

1. Put coconut milk in your slow cooker.
2. Add tapioca, vanilla and orange extract, stir, cover and cook on High for 2 hours.
3. Divide into bowls and serve for breakfast.
4. Enjoy!

Nutritional Value (Amount per Serving):

- Calories: 140
- Fat: 1
- Carbs: 3
- Protein: 5

Cornbread Casserole

Prep Time: 10 Minutes   Cook Time: 2 Hours And 30 Minutes   Serves: 6

Ingredients:

- 3 garlic cloves, minced
- 1 green bell pepper, chopped
- 1 yellow onion, chopped
- 15 ounces canned black beans, drained
- 15 ounces canned red kidney beans, drained
- 15 ounces canned pinto beans, drained
- 15 ounces canned tomatoes, chopped
- 10 ounces tomato sauce
- 10 ounces canned corn, drained
- 2 teaspoons chili powder
- 1 teaspoon hot sauce
- A pinch of salt and pepper
- 1/2 cup yellow corn meal
- 1/2 cup almond flour
- 1 and 1/4 teaspoons baking powder
- 1 tablespoon palm sugar
- 3/4 cup almond milk
- 1 tablespoon chia seeds
- 1 and 1/2 tablespoons vegetable oil
- Cooking spray

Directions:

1. Heat up a pan over medium high heat, add garlic, bell pepper and onions, brown them for 7 minutes and transfer them to your slow cooker after you've sprayed with cooking spray.
2. Add black beans, pinto beans, red kidney beans, tomatoes, tomato sauce, corn, chili powder, salt, pepper and hot sauce, stir, cover and cook on High for 1 hour.
3. Meanwhile, in a bowl, mix almond flour with cornmeal, baking powder,

sugar, milk, chia seeds and vegetable oil and stir really well.

4.Add this to the slow cooker and spread.

5.Cover slow cooker again and cook on High for 1 hour and 30 minutes more.

6.Leave your cornbread to cool down before slicing and serving.

7.Enjoy!

Nutritional Value (Amount per Serving):

- Calories: 240
- Fat: 4
- Carbs: 6
- Protein: 9

Apple Crumble

Prep Time: 10 Minutes   Cook Time: 4 Hours   Serves: 4

Ingredients:

- 1 cup granola
- 2 apples, peeled, cored and cut into chunks
- 1/8 cup maple syrup
- 2 tablespoons coconut butter
- 1/4 cup apple juice
- 1/2 teaspoon nutmeg, ground
- 1 teaspoon cinnamon, ground

Directions:

1. Put the apples in your slow cooker.
2. Add maple syrup, butter, apple juice, nutmeg and cinnamon.
3. Stir gently, sprinkle granola on top, cover and cook on Low for 4 hours.
4. Divide into bowls and serve.
5. Enjoy!

Nutritional Value (Amount per Serving):

- Calories: 160
- Fat: 1
- Carbs: 4
- Protein: 5

Blueberry Butter

Prep Time: 10 Minutes   Cook Time: 6 Hours   Serves: 12

Ingredients:

- 5 cups blueberries puree
- 2 teaspoons cinnamon powder
- Zest from 1 lemon
- 1 cup coconut sugar
- 1/2 teaspoon nutmeg, ground
- 1/4 teaspoon ginger, ground

Directions:

1. Put blueberries in your slow cooker, cover and cook on Low for 1 hour.
2. Stir your berries puree, cover and cook on Low for 4 hours more.
3. Add sugar, ginger, nutmeg and lemon zest, stir and cook on High uncovered for 1 hour more.
4. Divide into jars, cover them and keep in a cold place until you serve it for breakfast.
5. Enjoy!

Nutritional Value (Amount per Serving):

- Calories: 143
- Fat: 2
- Carbs: 3
- Protein: 4

Carrot Oatmeal

Prep Time: 10 Minutes   Cook Time: 7 Hours   Serves: 3

Ingredients:

- 2 cups coconut milk
- 1/2 cup old fashioned rolled oats
- 1 cup carrots, chopped
- 2 tablespoons agave nectar
- 1 teaspoon cardamom, ground
- A pinch of saffron
- Some chopped pistachios
- Cooking spray

Directions:

1. Spray your slow cooker with some cooking spray and add coconut milk.
2. Also, add oats, carrots, agave nectar, cardamom and saffron.
3. Stir, cover and cook on Low for 7 hours.
4. Stir oatmeal again, divide into bowls and serve with chopped pistachios on top.
5. Enjoy!

Nutritional Value (Amount per Serving):

- Calories: 140
- Fat: 2
- Carbs: 4
- Protein: 5

Breakfast Quinoa

Prep Time: 10 Minutes   Cook Time: 8 Hours   Serves: 4

Ingredients:

- 2 cups water
- 1 cup coconut milk
- 2 tablespoons maple syrup
- 1 cup quinoa, rinsed
- 1 teaspoon vanilla extract
- Berries for serving

Directions:

1. Put the water in your slow cooker.
2. Add milk, maple syrup and quinoa, stir, cover and cook on Low for 8 hours.
3. Fluff quinoa mix a bit, divide into bowls, add vanilla extract, stir and serve with your favorite berries on top.
4. Enjoy!

Nutritional Value (Amount per Serving):

- Calories: 120
- Fat: 2
- Carbs: 4
- Protein: 4

Pumpkin Butter

Prep Time: 10 Minutes   Cook Time: 4 Hours   Serves: 5

Ingredients:

- 2 teaspoons cinnamon powder
- 4 cups pumpkin puree
- 1 and 1/4 cup maple syrup
- 1/2 teaspoon nutmeg
- 1 teaspoon vanilla extract

Directions:

1. In your slow cooker, mix pumpkin puree with maple syrup and vanilla extract, stir, cover and cook on High for 4 hours.
2. Add cinnamon and nutmeg, stir, divide into jars and serve for breakfast!
3. Enjoy!

Nutritional Value (Amount per Serving):

- Calories: 120
- Fat: 2
- Carbs: 4
- Protein: 2

Mexican Breakfast

Ingredients:

- 1 cup brown rice
- 1 cup onion, chopped
- 2 cups veggie stock
- 1 red bell pepper, chopped
- 1 green bell pepper, chopped
- 4 ounces canned green chilies, chopped
- 15 ounces canned black beans, drained
- A pinch of salt
- Black pepper to the taste

For the salsa:

- 3 tablespoons lime juice
- 1 avocado, pitted, peeled and cubed
- 1/2 cup cilantro, chopped
- 1/2 cup green onions, chopped
- 1/2 cup tomato, chopped
- 1 poblano pepper, chopped
- 2 tablespoons olive oil
- 1/2 teaspoon cumin

Directions:

1. Put the stock in your slow cooker. Add rice, onions and beans, stir, cover and cook on High for 1 hour and 30 minutes.
2. Add chilies, red and green bell peppers, a pinch of salt and black pepper, stir, cover again and cook on High for 3 0 minutes more.
3. Meanwhile, in a bowl, mix avocado with green onions, tomato, poblano pepper, cilantro, oil, cumin, a pinch of salt, black pepper and lime juice and stir really well.
4. Divide rice mix into bowls; top each with the salsa you've just made and serve.

5.Enjoy!

Nutritional Value (Amount per Serving):

- Calories: 140
- Fat: 2
- Carbs: 5
- Protein: 5

Tofu Burrito

Prep Time: 10 Minutes   Cook Time: 8 Hours   Serves: 4

Ingredients:

- 15 ounces canned black beans, drained
- 2 tablespoons onions, chopped
- 7 ounces tofu, drained and crumbled
- 2 tablespoons green bell pepper, chopped
- 1/2 teaspoon turmeric
- 3/4 cup water
- 1/4 teaspoon smoked paprika
- 1/4 teaspoon cumin, ground
- 1/4 teaspoon chili powder
- A pinch of salt and black pepper
- 4 gluten free whole wheat tortillas serving
- Avocado, chopped for serving
- Salsa for serving

Directions:

1. Put black beans in your slow cooker.
2. Add onions, tofu, bell pepper, turmeric, water, paprika, cumin, chili powder, a pinch of salt and pepper, stir, cover and cook on Low for 8 hours.
3. Divide this on each tortilla, add avocado and salsa, wrap, arrange on plates and serve.
4. Enjoy!

Nutritional Value (Amount per Serving):

- Calories: 130
- Fat: 4
- Carbs: 5
- Protein: 4

Cherry Oatmeal

Ingredients:

- 2 cups almond milk
- 2 cups water
- 1 cup steel cut oats
- 2 tablespoons cocoa powder
- 1/3 cup cherries, pitted
- 1/4 cup maple syrup
- 1/2teaspoon almond extract

For the sauce:
- 2 tablespoons water
- 1 and 1/2 cups cherries, pitted and chopped
- 1/4 teaspoon almond extract

Directions:

1. Put the almond milk in your slow cooker.
2. Add 2 cups water, oats, cocoa powder, 1/3 cup cherries, maples syrup and 1/2 teaspoon almond extract.
3. Stir, cover and cook on Low for 8 hours.
4. In a small pan, mix 2 tablespoons water with 1 and 1/2 cups cherries and 1/4 teaspoon almond extract, stir well, bring to a simmer over medium heat and cook for 10 minutes until it thickens.
5. Divide oatmeal into breakfast bowls, top with the cherries sauce and serve.
6. Enjoy!

Nutritional Value (Amount per Serving):

- Calories: 150
- Fat: 1
- Carbs: 6
- Protein: 5

Carrot and Zucchini Breakfast

Prep Time: 10 Minutes   Cook Time: 8 Hours   Serves: 4

Ingredients:

- 1 and 1/2 cups almond milk
- 1/2 cup steel cut oats
- A pinch of nutmeg, ground
- 1 small zucchini, grated
- 1 carrot, grated
- A pinch of cloves, ground
- 2 tablespoons agave nectar
- 1/2 teaspoon cinnamon powder
- 1/4 cup pecans, chopped

Directions:

1. Put the milk in your slow cooker and mix with oats, zucchini, carrots, nutmeg, cloves, cinnamon and agave nectar.
2. Stir, cover and cook on Low for 8 hours.
3. Add pecans, stir gently, divide into bowls and serve right away.
4. Enjoy!

Nutritional Value (Amount per Serving):

- Calories: 120
- Fat: 1
- Carbs: 5
- Protein: 8

Quinoa and Cranberries Breakfast

Prep Time: 10 Minutes   Cook Time: 4 Hours   Serves: 4

Ingredients:

- 1/4 cup cranberries, dried
- 1/8 cup coconut flakes
- 1/8 cup almonds, sliced
- 3 teaspoons agave nectar
- 1 cup quinoa
- 3 cups water
- 1 teaspoon vanilla extract

Directions:

1. Put the water in your slow cooker.
2. Add quinoa, vanilla extract, cranberries, coconut flakes, agave nectar and almonds, stir, cover and cook on Low for 4 hours.
3. Fluff quinoa with a fork before dividing into bowls and serving.
4. Enjoy!

Nutritional Value (Amount per Serving):

- Calories: 120
- Fat: 2
- Carbs: 6
- Protein: 7

Banana Bread

Prep Time: 10 Minutes   Cook Time: 4 Hours   Serves: 6

Ingredients:

- 3 bananas, peeled and mashed
- 1 teaspoon baking powder
- 1/2 teaspoon baking soda
- 2 cups whole wheat flour
- 1 cup palm sugar
- 2 tablespoons flax meal + 1 tablespoon water
- 1/2 cup coconut butter, melted

Directions:

1. In a bowl, mix sugar with flour, baking soda and baking powder and stir.
2. Add flax meal mixed with the water, butter and bananas, stir really well and pour the mix into a greased round pan that fits your slow cooker.
3. Arrange the pan into your slow cooker, cover and cook on Low for 4 hours.
4. Leave your bread to cool down, slice and serve it for breakfast.
5. Enjoy!

Nutritional Value (Amount per Serving):

- Calories: 160
- Fat: 3
- Carbs: 7
- Protein: 6

Energy Bars

Prep Time: 10 Minutes   Cook Time: 4 Hours   Serves: 8

Ingredients:

- 1/2 teaspoon cinnamon
- 1 cup almond milk
- 1/3 cup quinoa
- 2 tablespoons chia seeds
- 1/3 cup apple, dried and chopped
- 1/2 cup raisins
- 2 tablespoons maple syrup
- 2 tablespoons almond butter, melted
- 1/3 cup almonds, roasted and chopped
- 2 tablespoons flax meal + 1 tablespoon water
- Cooking spray

Directions:

1. Grease your slow cooker with cooking spray and add a parchment paper inside.
2. In a bowl, mix melted almond butter with maple syrup and whisk really well.
3. Add cinnamon and almond milk and whisk everything.
4. Add flax meal mixed with water and stir well again.
5. Transfer this to your slow cooker, add quinoa, chia, apples and raisins, stir really well and press into the slow cooker.
6. Cover and cook on Low for 4 hours.
7. Take quinoa sheet out of the slow cooker using the parchment paper as handles, leave aside to cool down, slice and serve.
8. Enjoy!

Nutritional Value (Amount per Serving):

- Calories: 140
- Fat: 3
- Carbs: 6
- Protein: 5

Breakfast Buns

Prep Time: 10 Minutes   Cook Time: 2 Hours   Serves: 6

Ingredients:

- 6 tablespoons almond milk, hot
- 1/2 tablespoon coconut butter, melted
- 4 tablespoons maple syrup
- 1 teaspoon vanilla extract
- 2 and 1/4 teaspoons yeast
- 2 cups whole wheat flour
- Cooking spray

For the sauce:

- 1/4 cup pecans, chopped
- 2 tablespoons almond milk
- 2 tablespoons coconut butter, melted
- 4 tablespoons maple syrup

For the filling:

- 1/2 tablespoons coconut butter, melted
- 3 tablespoons maple syrup
- 1 and 1/2 teaspoons cinnamon powder

Directions:

1. In a bowl, mix 6 tablespoons milk with 1/2 tablespoon butter, 1 teaspoon vanilla extract and 4 tablespoons maple syrup, stir well and heat up in your microwave for a few seconds.
2. Add flour and yeast, knead really well until you obtain a dough and leave aside for now.
3. In a bowl, mix 2 tablespoons almond milk with 2 tablespoons coconut butter, 4 tablespoons maple syrup and pecans and stir really well.
4. In another bowl, mix 1/2 tablespoon coconut butter with 3 tablespoons maple syrup and cinnamon powder and stir well.
5. Divide your dough into 12 rectangles and brush each with the cinnamon filling.

6. Roll and shape 12 balls and dip each in the maple syrup and pecans sauce you've made.
7. Grease your slow cooker with the cooking spray and arrange your sweet buns in it.
8. Cover and cook on Low for 2 hours.
9. Leave your buns to cool down completely before serving.
10. Enjoy!

Nutritional Value (Amount per Serving):

- Calories: 200
- Fat: 4
- Carbs: 7
- Protein: 5

Fruity Breakfast

Prep Time: 10 Minutes   Cook Time: 8 Hours   Serves: 6

Ingredients:

- 1 cup apricots, dried and chopped
- 3/4 cup red quinoa
- 3/4 cup steel cut oats
- 2 tablespoons agave nectar
- 1/2 teaspoon vanilla bean paste
- 3/4 cup hazelnuts, toasted and chopped
- 6 cups water
- Chopped hazelnuts for serving

Directions:

1. In a bowl, mix quinoa with oats, vanilla bean paste, apricots, hazelnuts, agave nectar and water and stir well.
2. Pour this into your slow cooker, cover and cook on Low for 8 hours.
3. Stir again everything, divide into bowls and serve with more chopped hazelnuts on top.
4. Enjoy!

Nutritional Value (Amount per Serving):

- Calories: 251
- Fat: 4
- Carbs: 10
- Protein: 7

Creamy Quinoa

Prep Time: 10 Minutes   Cook Time: 2 Hours   Serves: 4

Ingredients:

- 3 cups almond milk
- 1 cup quinoa
- 1 apple, cored, peeled and chopped
- 1/4 cup pepitas
- 4 dates, chopped
- 1/4 teaspoon nutmeg, ground
- 2 teaspoons cinnamon powder
- 1 teaspoon vanilla extract

Directions:

1. Put the milk in your slow cooker.
2. Add quinoa, apple, dates, pepitas, cinnamon, nutmeg and vanilla.
3. Stir, cover and cook on High for 2 hours.
4. Divide into bowls and serve for breakfast.
5. Enjoy!

Nutritional Value (Amount per Serving):

- Calories: 130
- Fat: 3
- Carbs: 10
- Protein: 5

CHAPTER 3: SIDE DISH

Creamy Corn

Prep Time: 10 Minutes   Cook Time: 3 Hours   Serves: 6

Ingredients:

- 50 ounces corn
- 1 cup almond milk
- 1 tablespoon stevia
- 8 ounces coconut cream
- A pinch of white pepper

Directions:

1. In your slow cooker, mix corn with almond milk, stevia, cream and white pepper, toss, cover and cook on High for 3 hours.
2. Divide between plates and serve as a side dish.
3. Enjoy!

Nutritional Value (Amount per Serving):

- Calories: 200
- Fat: 5
- Carbs: 12
- Protein: 4

Potatoes Side Dish

Prep Time: 10 Minutes   Cook Time: 3 Hours   Serves: 12

Ingredients:

- 2 tablespoons olive oil
- 3 pounds new potatoes, halved
- 7 garlic cloves, minced
- 1 tablespoon rosemary, chopped
- A pinch of salt and black pepper

Directions:

1. In your slow cooker, mix oil with potatoes, garlic, rosemary, salt and pepper, toss, cover and cook on High for 3 hours.
2. Divide between plates and serve as a side dish.
3. Enjoy!

Nutritional Value (Amount per Serving):

- Calories: 102
- Fat: 2
- Carbs: 18
- Protein: 2

Beets And Carrots

Prep Time: 10 Minutes   Cook Time: 7 Hours   Serves: 8

Ingredients:

- 2 tablespoons stevia
- 3/4 cup pomegranate juice
- 2 teaspoons ginger, grated
- 2 and $1/2 pounds beets, peeled and cut into wedges
- 12 ounces carrots, cut into medium wedges

Directions:

1. In your slow cooker, mix beets with carrots, ginger, stevia and pomegranate juice, toss, cover and cook on Low for 7 hours.
2. Divide between plates and serve as a side dish.
3. Enjoy!

Nutritional Value (Amount per Serving):

- Calories: 125
- Fat: 0
- Carbs: 28
- Protein: 3

Potatoes Mix

Prep Time: 10 Minutes   Cook Time: 7 Hours   Serves: 10

Ingredients:

- 2 green apples, cored and cut into wedges
- 3 pounds sweet potatoes, peeled and cut into medium wedges
- 1 cup coconut cream
- 1/2 cup dried cherries
- 1 cup apple butter
- 1 and 1/2 teaspoon pumpkin pie spice

Directions:

1. In your slow cooker, mix sweet potatoes with green apples, cream, cherries, apple butter and spice, toss, cover and cook on Low for 7 hours.
2. Toss, divide between plates and serve as a side dish.
3. Enjoy!

Nutritional Value (Amount per Serving):

- Calories: 351
- Fat: 8
- Carbs: 48
- Protein: 2

Cauliflower and Broccoli Side Dish

Prep Time: 10 Minutes   Cook Time: 3 Hours   Serves: 10

Ingredients:

- 4 cups broccoli florets
- 4 cups cauliflower florets
- 14 ounces tomato paste
- 1 yellow onion, chopped
- 1 teaspoon thyme, dried
- Salt and black pepper to the taste
- 1/2 cup almonds, sliced

Directions:

1. In your slow cooker, mix broccoli with cauliflower, tomato paste, onion, thyme, salt and pepper, toss, cover and cook on High for 3 hours.
2. Add almonds, toss, divide between plates and serve as a side dish.
3. Enjoy!

Nutritional Value (Amount per Serving):

- Calories: 177
- Fat: 12
- Carbs: 10
- Protein: 7

Acorn Squash and Great Sauce

Prep Time: 10 Minutes   Cook Time: 6 Hours   Serves: 4

Ingredients:

- 2 acorn squash, halved, deseeded and cut into medium wedges
- 1/4 cup raisins
- 16 ounces cranberry sauce
- 1/4 cup orange marmalade
- A pinch of salt and black pepper
- 1/4 teaspoon cinnamon powder

Directions:

1. In your slow cooker, mix squash with raisins, cranberry sauce, orange marmalade, salt, pepper and cinnamon powder, toss, cover and cook on Low for 6 hours.
2. Stir again, divide between plates and serve as a side dish.
3. Enjoy!

Nutritional Value (Amount per Serving):

- Calories: 325
- Fat: 6
- Carbs: 28
- Protein: 3

Brussels SproutsM

Prep Time: 10 Minutes   Cook Time: 3 Hours   Serves: 12

Ingredients:

- 1 cup red onion, chopped
- 2 pounds Brussels sprouts, trimmed and halved
- A pinch of salt and black pepper
- 1/4 cup apple juice
- 3 tablespoons olive oil
- 1/4 cup maple syrup
- 1 tablespoon thyme, chopped

Directions:

1. In your slow cooker, mix Brussels sprouts with onion, salt, pepper and apple juice, toss, cover and cook on Low for 3 hours.
2. In a bowl, mix maple syrup with oil and thyme, whisk really well and add over Brussels sprouts.
3. Toss well, divide between plates and serve as a side dish.
4. Enjoy!

Nutritional Value (Amount per Serving):

- Calories: 100
- Fat: 4
- Carbs: 14
- Protein: 3

Mushroom and Peas Risotto

Prep Time: 10 Minutes   Cook Time: 1 Hour And 30 Minutes   Serves: 8

Ingredients:

- 1 shallot, chopped
- 8 ounces white mushrooms, sliced
- 3 tablespoons olive oil
- 1 teaspoon garlic, minced
- 1 and 3/4 cup white rice
- 4 cups veggie stock
- 1 cup peas
- Salt and black pepper to the taste

Directions:

1. In your slow cooker, mix oil with shallot, mushrooms, garlic, rice, stock, peas, salt and pepper, stir, cover and cook on High for 1 hour and 30 minutes.
2. Stir risotto one more time, divide between plates and serve as a side dish.
3. Enjoy!

Nutritional Value (Amount per Serving):

- Calories: 254
- Fat: 7
- Carbs: 27
- Protein: 7

Squash and Spinach Mix

Prep Time: 10 Minutes   Cook Time: 3 Hours And 30 Minutes   Serves: 12

Ingredients:

- 10 ounces spinach, torn
- 2 pounds butternut squash, peeled and cubed
- 1 cup barley
- 1 yellow onion, chopped
- 14 ounces veggie stock
- 1/2 cup water
- A pinch of salt and black pepper to the taste
- 3 garlic cloves, minced

Directions:

1. In your slow cooker, mix squash with spinach, barley, onion, stock, water, salt, pepper and garlic, toss, cover and cook on High for 3 hours and 30 minutes.
2. Divide squash mix on plates and serve as a side dish.
3. Enjoy!

Nutritional Value (Amount per Serving):

- Calories: 196
- Fat: 3
- Carbs: 36
- Protein: 7

Flavored Beets

Prep Time: 10 Minutes   Cook Time: 8 Hours   Serves: 6

Ingredients:

- 6 beets, peeled and cut into wedges
- A pinch of sea salt
- Black pepper to the taste
- 2 tablespoons lemon juice
- 2 tablespoons olive oil
- 2 tablespoons agave nectar
- 1 tablespoon cider vinegar
- 1/2 teaspoon lemon rind, grated
- 2 rosemary sprigs

Directions:

1. Put the beets in your slow cooker.
2. Add a pinch of salt, black pepper, lemon juice, oil, agave nectar, rosemary and vinegar. Stir everything, cover and cook on Low for 8 hours.
3. Add lemon rind, stir, divide between plates and serve.
4. Enjoy!

Nutritional Value (Amount per Serving):

- Calories: 120
- Fat: 1
- Carbs: 6
- Protein: 6

Sweet Potatoes Side Dish

Prep Time: 10 Minutes   Cook Time: 3 Hours   Serves: 10

Ingredients:

- 4 pounds sweet potatoes, thinly sliced
- 3 tablespoons stevia
- 1/2 cup orange juice
- A pinch of salt and black pepper
- 1/2 teaspoon thyme, dried
- 1/2 teaspoon sage, dried
- 2 tablespoons olive oil

Directions:

1. Arrange potato slices on the bottom of your slow cooker.
2. In a bowl, mix orange juice with salt, pepper, stevia, thyme, sage and oil and whisk well.
3. Add this over potatoes, cover slow cooker and cook on High for 3 hours.
4. Divide between plates and serve as a side dish.
5. Enjoy!

Nutritional Value (Amount per Serving):

- Calories: 189
- Fat: 4
- Carbs: 36
- Protein: 4

Rustic Mashed Potatoes

Prep Time: 10 Minutes   Cook Time: 4 Hours   Serves: 6

Ingredients:

- 6 garlic cloves, peeled
- 3 pounds gold potatoes, peeled and cubed
- 1 bay leaf
- 1 cup coconut milk
- 28 ounces veggie stock
- 3 tablespoons olive oil
- Salt and black pepper to the taste

Directions:

1. In your slow cooker, mix potatoes with stock, bay leaf, garlic, salt and pepper, cover and cook on High for 4 hours.
2. Drain potatoes and garlic, return them to your slow cooker and mash using a potato masher.
3. Add oil and coconut milk, whisk well, divide between plates and serve as a side dish.
4. Enjoy!

Nutritional Value (Amount per Serving):

- Calories: 135
- Fat: 5
- Carbs: 20
- Protein: 3

Barley and Squash Gratin

Prep Time: 10 Minutes   Cook Time: 7 Hours   Serves: 12

Ingredients:

- 2 pounds butternut squash, peeled and cubed
- 1 yellow onion, cut into medium wedges
- 10 ounces spinach
- 1 cup barley
- 14 ounces veggie stock
- 1/2 cup water
- A pinch of salt
- Black pepper to the taste
- 3 garlic cloves, minced

Directions:

1. Put squash pieces in your slow cooker.
2. Add barley, spinach, stock, water, onion, garlic, salt and pepper, stir, cover and cook on Low for 7 hours.
3. Stir this mix again, divide between plates and serve.
4. Enjoy!

Nutritional Value (Amount per Serving):

- Calories: 200
- Fat: 3
- Carbs: 13
- Protein: 7

Pilaf

Prep Time: 10 Minutes   Cook Time: 7 Hours   Serves: 12

Ingredients:

- 1/2 cup wild rice
- 1/2cup barley
- 2/3 cup wheat berries
- 27 ounces veggie stock
- 2 cups baby lima beans
- 1 red bell pepper, chopped
- 1 yellow onion, chopped
- 1 tablespoon olive oil
- A pinch of salt and black pepper
- 1 teaspoon sage, dried and crushed
- 4 garlic cloves, minced

Directions:

1. In your slow cooker, mix rice with barley, wheat berries, lima beans, bell pepper, onion, oil, salt, pepper, sage and garlic, stir, cover and cook on Low for 7 hours.
2. Stir one more time, divide between plates and serve as a side dish.
3. Enjoy!

Nutritional Value (Amount per Serving):

- Calories: 168
- Fat: 5
- Carbs: 25
- Protein: 6

Sweet Potatoes Dish

Prep Time: 10 Minutes   Cook Time: 6 Hours   Serves: 6

Ingredients:

- 4 pounds sweet potatoes, peeled and sliced
- 1/2 cup orange juice
- 3 tablespoons palm sugar
- 1/2 teaspoon thyme, dried
- A pinch of sea salt
- Black pepper to the taste
- 1/2 teaspoon sage, dried
- 2 tablespoons olive oil

Directions:

1. Put the oil in your slow cooker and add sweet potato slices.
2. In a bowl, mix orange juice with palm sugar, thyme, sage, a pinch of salt and black pepper and whisk well.
3. Add this over potatoes, toss to coat, cover slow cooker and cook on Low for 6 hours.
4. Stir sweet potatoes mix again, divide between plates and serve.
5. Enjoy!

Nutritional Value (Amount per Serving):

- Calories: 160
- Fat: 3
- Carbs: 6
- Protein: 9

Black Eyed Peas

Prep Time: 10 Minutes   Cook Time: 8 Hours   Serves: 6

Ingredients:

- 3 cups black eyed peas
- A pinch of salt
- Black pepper to the taste
- 2 cups veggie stock
- 2 tablespoons jalapeno peppers, chopped
- 2 cups sweet onion, chopped
- 1/2 teaspoon thyme, dried
- 4 garlic cloves, minced
- 1 bay leaf
- Hot sauce to the taste

Directions:

1. Put the peas in your slow cooker.
2. Add a pinch of salt, black pepper, stock, jalapenos, onion, garlic, thyme and bay leaf.
3. Stir everything, cover and cook on Low for 8 hours.
4. Drizzle hot sauce over peas, stir gently, divide between plates and serve.
5. Enjoy!

Nutritional Value (Amount per Serving):

- Calories: 130
- Fat: 2
- Carbs: 7
- Protein: 7

Orange Carrots

Ingredients:

- 3 pounds carrots, peeled and cut into medium pieces
- A pinch of sea salt
- Black pepper to the taste
- 2 tablespoons water 1/2 cup agave nectar
- 2 tablespoons olive oil
- 1/2 teaspoon orange rind, grated

Directions:

1. Put the oil in your slow cooker and add the carrots.
2. In a bowl mix agave nectar with water and whisk well.
3. Add this to your slow cooker as well.
4. Also, add a pinch of sea salt and black pepper, stir gently everything, cover and cook on Low for 8 hours.
5. Sprinkle orange rind all over, stir gently, divide on plates and serve.
6. Enjoy!

Nutritional Value (Amount per Serving):

- Calories: 140
- Fat: 2
- Carbs: 4
- Protein: 6

Italian Veggie Side Dish

Prep Time: 10 Minutes   Cook Time: 6 Hours   Serves: 8

Ingredients:

- 38 ounces canned cannellini beans, drained
- 1 yellow onion, chopped
- 1/4 cup basil pesto
- 19 ounces canned fava beans, drained
- 4 garlic cloves, minced
- 1 and 1/2 teaspoon Italian seasoning, dried and crushed
- 1 tomato, chopped
- 15 ounces already cooked polenta, cut into medium pieces
- 2 cups spinach
- 1 cup radicchio, torn

Directions:

1. In your slow cooker, mix cannellini beans with fava beans, basil pesto, onion, garlic, Italian seasoning, polenta, tomato, spinach and radicchio, toss, cover and cook on Low for 6 hours.
2. Divide between plates and serve as a side dish.
3. Enjoy!

Nutritional Value (Amount per Serving):

- Calories: 364
- Fat: 12
- Carbs: 45
- Protein: 21

Wild Rice Mix

Prep Time: 10 Minutes   Cook Time: 6 Hours   Serves: 12

Ingredients:

- 40 ounces veggie stock
- 2 and 1/2 cups wild rice
- 1 cup carrot, shredded
- 4 ounces mushrooms, sliced
- 2 tablespoons olive oil
- 2 teaspoons marjoram, dried and crushed
- Salt and black pepper to the taste
- 2/3 cup dried cherries
- 1/2 cup pecans, toasted and chopped
- 2/3 cup green onions, chopped

Directions:

1. In your slow cooker, mix stock with wild rice, carrot, mushrooms, oil, marjoram, salt, pepper, cherries, pecans and green onions, toss, cover and cook on Low for 6 hours.
2. Stir wild rice one more time, divide between plates and serve as a side dish.
3. Enjoy!

Nutritional Value (Amount per Serving):

- Calories: 169
- Fat: 5
- Carbs: 28
- Protein: 5

Glazed Carrots

Prep Time: 10 Minutes   Cook Time: 4 Hours   Serves: 10

Ingredients:

- 1 pound parsnips, cut into medium chunks
- 2 pounds carrots, cut into medium chunks
- 2 tablespoons orange peel, shredded
- 1 cup orange juice
- 1/2 cup orange marmalade
- 1/2 cup veggie stock
- 1 tablespoon tapioca, crushed
- A pinch of salt and black pepper
- 3 tablespoons olive oil
- 1/4 cup parsley, chopped

Directions:

1. In your slow cooker, mix parsnips with carrots.
2. In a bowl, mix orange peel with orange juice, stock, orange marmalade, tapioca, salt and pepper, whisk and add over carrots.
3. Cover slow cooker and cook everything on High for 4 hours.
4. Add parsley, toss, divide between plates and serve as a side dish.
5. Enjoy!

Nutritional Value (Amount per Serving):

- Calories: 159
- Fat: 4
- Carbs: 30
- Protein: 2

CHAPTER 4: MAIN DISH

Beans, Carrots and Spinach Side Dish

Prep Time: 10 Minutes   Cook Time: 4 Hours   Serves: 6

Ingredients:

- 5 carrots, sliced
- 1 and 1/2 cups great northern beans, dried, soaked overnight and drained
- 2 garlic cloves, minced
- 1 yellow onion, chopped
- Salt and black pepper to the taste
- 1/2 teaspoon oregano, dried
- 5 ounces baby spinach
- 4 and 1/2 cups veggie stock
- 2 teaspoons lemon peel, grated
- 3 tablespoons lemon juice
- 1 avocado, pitted, peeled and chopped
- 3/4 cup tofu, firm, pressed, drained and crumbled
- 1/4 cup pistachios, chopped

Directions:

1. In your slow cooker, mix beans with onion, carrots, garlic, salt, pepper, oregano and veggie stock, stir, cover and cook on High for 4 hours.
2. Drain beans mix, return to your slow cooker and reserve 1/4 cup cooking liquid.
3. Add spinach, lemon juice and lemon peel, stir and leave aside for 5 minutes.
4. Transfer beans, carrots and spinach mixture to a bowl, add pistachios, avocado, tofu and reserve cooking liquid, toss, divide between plates and serve as a side dish.
5. Enjoy!

Nutritional Value (Amount per Serving):

- Calories: 319
- Fat: 8
- Carbs: 43
- Protein: 17

Beans and Lentils

Prep Time: 10 Minutes   Cook Time: 7 Hours And 10 Minutes   Serves: 6

Ingredients:

- 2 tablespoons thyme, chopped
- 1 tablespoon olive oil
- 1 cup yellow onion, chopped
- 5 cups water 5 garlic cloves, minced
- 3 tablespoons cider vinegar
- 1/2 cup tomato paste
- 1/2 cup maple syrup
- 3 tablespoons soy sauce
- 2 tablespoons Korean red chili paste
- 2 tablespoons dry mustard
- 1 and 1/2 cups great northern beans
- 1/2 cup red lentils

Directions:

1. Heat up a pan with the oil over medium high heat, add onion, stir and cook for 4 minutes.
2. Add garlic, thyme, vinegar and tomato paste, stir, cook for 5 minutes more and transfer to your slow cooker.
3. Add lentils and beans to your slow cooker and stir.
4. Also add water, maple syrup, mustard, chili paste and soy sauce, stir, cover and cook on High for 7 hours.
5. Stir beans mix again, divide between plates and serve.
6. Enjoy!

Nutritional Value (Amount per Serving):

- Calories: 160
- Fat: 2
- Carbs: 7
- Protein: 8

Eggplant and Kale Mix

Prep Time: 10 Minutes   Cook Time: 2 Hours   Serves: 6

Ingredients:

- 14 ounces canned roasted tomatoes and garlic
- 4 cups eggplant, cubed
- 1 yellow bell pepper, chopped
- 1 red onion, cut into medium wedges
- 4 cups kale leaves
- 2 tablespoons olive oil
- 1 teaspoon mustard
- 3 tablespoons red vinegar
- 1 garlic clove, minced
- A pinch of salt and black pepper
- 1/ 2cup basil, chopped

Directions:

1. In your slow cooker, mix eggplant cubes with canned tomatoes, bell pepper and onion, toss, cover and cook on High for 2 hours.
2. Add kale, toss, cover slow cooker and leave aside for now.
3. Meanwhile, in a bowl, mix oil with vinegar, mustard, garlic, salt and pepper and whisk well.
4. Add this over eggplant mix, also add basil, toss, divide between plates and serve as a side dish.
5. Enjoy!

Nutritional Value (Amount per Serving):

- Calories: 251
- Fat: 9
- Carbs: 34
- Protein: 8

Mashed Potatoes

Prep Time: 10 Minutes   Cook Time: 6 Hours   Serves: 12

Ingredients:

- 3 pounds russet potatoes, peeled and cubed
- 6 garlic cloves, chopped
- 28 ounces veggie stock
- 1 bay leaf
- 1 cup coconut milk
- 1/4 cup coconut butter
- A pinch of sea salt
- White pepper to the taste

Directions:

1. Put potatoes in your slow cooker.
2. Add stock, garlic and bay leaf, stir, cover and cook on Low for 6 hours.
3. Drain potatoes, discard bay leaf, return them to your slow cooker and mash using a potato masher.
4. Meanwhile, put the coconut milk in a pot, stir and heat up over medium heat.
5. Add coconut butter and stir until it dissolves.
6. Add this to your mashed potatoes, season with a pinch of salt and white pepper, stir well, divide between plates and serve as a side dish.
7. Enjoy!

Nutritional Value (Amount per Serving):

- Calories: 1535
- Fat: 4
- Carbs: 10
- Protein: 4

Chickpeas and Veggies

Prep Time: 10 Minutes   Cook Time: 8 Hour   Serves: 6

Ingredients:

- 30 ounces canned chickpeas, drained
- 2 tablespoons olive oil
- 2 tablespoons rosemary, chopped
- A pinch of salt and black pepper
- 2 cups cherry tomatoes, halved
- 2 garlic cloves, minced
- 1 cup corn
- 1 pound baby potatoes, peeled and halved
- 12 small baby carrots, peeled
- 28 ounces veggie stock
- 1 yellow onion, cut into medium wedges
- 4 cups baby spinach
- 8 ounces zucchini, sliced

Directions:

1. In your slow cooker, mix chickpeas with oil, rosemary, salt, pepper, cherry tomatoes, garlic, corn, baby potatoes, baby carrots, onion, zucchini, spinach and stock, stir, cover and cook on Low for 8 hours.
2. Divide everything between plates and serve as a side dish.
3. Enjoy!

Nutritional Value (Amount per Serving):

- Calories: 273
- Fat: 7
- Carbs: 38
- Protein: 12

Scalloped Potatoes

Prep Time: 10 Minutes   Cook Time: 4 Hours   Serves: 8

Ingredients:

- Cooking spray
- 2 pounds gold potatoes, halved and sliced
- 1 yellow onion, cut into medium wedges
- 10 ounces canned vegan potato cream soup
- 8 ounces coconut milk
- 1 cup tofu, crumbled
- 1/2 cup veggie stock
- Salt and black pepper to the taste
- 1 tablespoons parsley, chopped

Directions:

1. Coat your slow cooker with cooking spray and arrange half of the potatoes on the bottom.
2. Layer onion wedges, half of the vegan cream soup, coconut milk, tofu, stock, salt and pepper.
3. Add the rest of the potatoes, onion wedges, cream, coconut milk, tofu and stock, cover and cook on High for 4 hours.
4. Sprinkle parsley on top, divide scalloped potatoes between plates and serve as a side dish.
5. Enjoy!

Nutritional Value (Amount per Serving):

- Calories: 306
- Fat: 14
- Carbs: 30
- Protein: 12

Mexican Black Beans

Prep Time: 10 Minutes   Cook Time: 10 Hours   Serves: 4

Ingredients:

- 1 pound black beans, soaked overnight and drained
- A pinch of sea salt
- Black pepper to the taste
- 3 cups veggie stock
- 2 cups yellow onion, chopped
- 1 tablespoon canned chipotle chili pepper in adobo sauce
- 4 garlic cloves, minced
- 1 tablespoon lime juice
- 1/2 cup cilantro, chopped
- 1/2 cup pumpkin seeds

Directions:

1. Put the beans in your slow cooker.
2. Add a pinch of salt, black pepper, onion, stock, garlic and chipotle chili in adobo sauce.
3. Stir, cover and cook on Low for 10 hours.
4. Add lime juice and mash beans a bit using a potato masher.
5. Add cilantro, stir gently, divide between plates and serve with pumpkin seeds on top.
6. Enjoy!

Nutritional Value (Amount per Serving):

- Calories: 150
- Fat: 3
- Carbs: 7
- Protein: 5

Collard Greens

Prep Time: 10 Minutes   Cook Time: 4 Hours And 5 Minutes   Serves: 4

Ingredients:

- 1 tablespoons olive oil
- 1 cup yellow onion, chopped
- 16 ounces collard greens
- 2 garlic cloves, minced
- A pinch of sea salt
- Black pepper to the taste
- 14 ounces veggie stock
- 1 bay leaf
- 1 tablespoon agave nectar
- 3 tablespoon balsamic vinegar

Directions:

1. Heat up a pan with the oil over medium high heat, add onion, stir and cook for 3 minutes. Add collard greens, stir, cook for 2 minutes more and transfer to your slow cooker.
2. Add garlic, salt, pepper, stock and bay leaf, stir, cover and cook on Low for 4 hours.
3. In a bowl, mix vinegar with agave nectar and whisk well.
4. Add this to collard greens, stir, divide between plates and serve.
5. Enjoy!

Nutritional Value (Amount per Serving):

- Calories: 130
- Fat: 1
- Carbs: 5
- Protein: 3

Wild Rice

Prep Time: 10 Minutes   Cook Time: 6 Hours   Serves: 12

Ingredients:

- 42 ounces veggie stock
- 1 cup carrot, shredded
- 2 and 1/2 cups wild rice
- 4 ounces mushrooms, sliced
- 2 tablespoons olive oil
- 2 teaspoons marjoram, dried
- A pinch of sea salt
- Black pepper to the taste
- 2/3 cup cherries, dried
- 1/2 cup pecans, chopped
- 2/3 cup green onions, chopped

Directions:

1. Put the stock in your slow cooker.
2. Add rice, carrots, mushrooms, oil, salt, pepper marjoram.
3. Stir, cover and cook on Low for 6 hours.
4. Add cherries and green onions, stir, cover slow cooker and leave it aside for 10 minutes.
5. Divide wild rice between plates and serve with chopped pecans on top.
6. Enjoy!

Nutritional Value (Amount per Serving):

- Calories: 140
- Fat: 2
- Carbs: 6
- Protein: 7

Thai Veggie Mix

Prep Time: 10 Minutes   Cook Time: 3 Hours   Serves: 8

Ingredients:

- 8 ounces yellow summer squash, peeled and roughly chopped
- 12 ounces zucchini, halved and sliced
- 2 cups button mushrooms, quartered
- 1 red sweet potatoes, chopped
- 2 leeks, sliced
- 2 tablespoons veggie stock
- 2 garlic cloves, minced
- 2 tablespoon Thai red curry paste
- 1 tablespoon ginger, grated
- 1/3 cup coconut milk
- 1/4cup basil, chopped

Directions:

1. In your slow cooker, mix zucchini with summer squash, mushrooms, red pepper, leeks, garlic, stock, curry paste, ginger, coconut milk and basil, toss, cover and cook on Low for 3 hours.
2. Stir your Thai mix one more time, divide between plates and serve as a side dish.
3. Enjoy!

Nutritional Value (Amount per Serving):

- Calories: 69
- Fat: 2
- Carbs: 8
- Protein: 2

CHAPTER 5: SNACK AND APPETIZER

Chipotle Tacos

Prep Time: 10 Minutes   Cook Time: 4 Hours   Serves: 4

Ingredients:

- 30 ounces canned pinto beans, drained
- 3/4 cup chili sauce
- 3 ounces chipotle pepper in adobo sauce, chopped
- 1 cup corn
- 6 ounces tomato paste
- 1 tablespoon cocoa powder
- 1/2 teaspoon cinnamon, ground
- 1 teaspoon cumin, ground
- 8 vegan taco shells
- Chopped avocado, for serving

Directions:

1. Put the beans in your slow cooker.
2. Add chili sauce, chipotle pepper, corn, tomato paste, cocoa powder, cinnamon and cumin.
3. Stir, cover and cook on Low for 4 hours. Divide beans and chopped avocado into taco shells and serve them.
4. Enjoy!

Nutritional Value (Amount per Serving):

- Calories: 342
- Fat: 3
- Carbs: 12
- Protein: 10

Spinach Dip

Prep Time: 10 Minutes   Cook Time: 4 Hours   Serves: 12

Ingredients:

- 8 ounces baby spinach
- 1 small yellow onion, chopped
- 8 ounces vegan cashew mozzarella, shredded
- 8 ounces tofu, cubed
- 1 cup vegan cashew parmesan cheese, grated
- 1 tablespoon garlic, minced
- A pinch of cayenne pepper
- A pinch of sea salt
- Black pepper to the taste

Directions:

1. Put spinach in your slow cooker. Add onion, cashew mozzarella, tofu, cashew parmesan, salt, pepper, cayenne and garlic.
2. Stir, cover and cook on Low for 2 hours.
3. Stir your dip well, cover and cook on Low for 2 more hours.
4. Divide your spinach dip into bowls and serve.
5. Enjoy!

Nutritional Value (Amount per Serving):

- Calories: 200
- Fat: 3
- Carbs: 6
- Protein: 8

Sweet and Spicy Nuts

Prep Time: 10 Minutes   **Cook Time: 2 Hours**   **Serves: 20**

Ingredients:

- 1 cup almonds, toasted
- 1 cup cashews
- 1 cup pecans, halved and toasted
- 1 cup hazelnuts, toasted and peeled
- 1/2 cup palm sugar
- 1 teaspoon ginger, grated
- 1/3 cup coconut butter, melted
- 1/2 teaspoon cinnamon powder
- 1/4 teaspoon cloves, ground
- A pinch of salt
- A pinch of cayenne pepper

Directions:

1. Put almonds, pecans, cashews and hazelnuts in your slow cooker.
2. Add palm sugar, coconut butter, ginger, salt, cayenne, cloves and cinnamon.
3. Stir well, cover and cook on Low for 2 hours.
4. Divide into bowls and serve as a snack.
5. Enjoy!

Nutritional Value (Amount per Serving):

- Calories: 110
- Fat: 3
- Carbs: 5
- Protein: 5

Corn Dip

Prep Time: 10 Minutes   Cook Time: 2 Hours And 15 Minutes   Serves: 8

Ingredients:

- 2 jalapenos, chopped
- 45 ounces canned corn kernels, drained
- 1/2 cup coconut milk
- 1 and 1/4 cups cashew cheese, shredded
- A pinch of sea salt
- Black pepper to the taste
- 2 tablespoons chives, chopped
- 8 ounces tofu, cubed

Directions:

1. In your slow cooker, mix coconut milk with cashew cheese, corn, jalapenos, tofu, salt and pepper, stir, cover and cook on Low for 2 hours.
2. Stir your corn dip really well, cover slow cooker again and cook on High for 15 minutes.
3. Divide into bowls, sprinkle chives on top and serve as a vegan snack!
4. Enjoy!

Nutritional Value (Amount per Serving):

- Calories: 150
- Fat: 3
- Carbs: 8
- Protein: 10

Butternut Squash Spread

Prep Time: 10 Minutes   Cook Time: 6 Hours   Serves: 4

Ingredients:

- 1/2 cup butternut squash, peeled and cubed
- 1/2 cup canned white beans, drained
- 1 tablespoon water
- 2 tablespoons coconut milk
- A pinch of rosemary, dried
- A pinch of sage, dried
- A pinch of salt and black pepper

Directions:

1. In your slow cooker, mix beans with squash, water, coconut milk, sage, rosemary, salt and pepper, toss, cover and cook on Low for 6 hours.
2. Blend using an immersion blender, divide into bowls and serve cold as a party spread.
3. Enjoy!

Nutritional Value (Amount per Serving):

- Calories: 182
- Fat: 5
- Carbs: 12
- Protein: 5

Cashew and White Bean Spread

Prep Time: 10 Minutes   Cook Time: 7 Hours   Serves: 4

Ingredients:

- 1/2 cup white beans, dried
- 2 tablespoons cashews, soaked for 12 hours and blended
- 1 teaspoon apple cider vinegar
- 1 cup veggie stock
- 1 tablespoon water

Directions:

1. In your slow cooker, mix beans with cashews and stock, stir, cover and cook on Low for 6 hours.
2. Drain, transfer to your food processor, add vinegar and water, pulse well, divide into bowls and serve as a spread.
3. Enjoy!

Nutritional Value (Amount per Serving):

- Calories: 221
- Fat: 6
- Carbs: 19
- Protein: 3

Vegan Rolls

Prep Time: 10 Minutes   Cook Time: 8 Hours   Serves: 4

Ingredients:

- 1 cup brown lentils, cooked
- 1 green cabbage head, leaves separated
- 1/2 cup onion, chopped
- 1 cup brown rice, already cooked
- 2 ounces white mushrooms, chopped
- 1/4 cup pine nuts, toasted
- 1/4cup raisins
- 2 garlic cloves, minced
- 2 tablespoons dill, chopped
- 1 tablespoon olive oil
- 25 ounces marinara sauce
- A pinch of salt and black pepper
- 1/4 cup water

Directions:

1. In a bowl, mix lentils with onion, rice, mushrooms, pine nuts, raisins, garlic, dill, salt and pepper and whisk well.
2. Arrange cabbage leaves on a working surface, divide lentils mix and wrap them well.
3. Add marinara sauce and water to your slow cooker and stir.
4. Add cabbage rolls, cover and cook on Low for 8 hours.
5. Arrange cabbage rolls on a platter, drizzle sauce all over and serve.
6. Enjoy!

Nutritional Value (Amount per Serving):

- Calories: 261
- Fat: 6
- Carbs: 12
- Protein: 3

Colored Stuffed Bell Peppers

Prep Time: 10 Minutes   Cook Time: 4 Hours   Serves: 5

Ingredients:

- 1 yellow onion, chopped
- 2 teaspoons olive oil
- 2 celery ribs, chopped
- 1 tablespoon chili powder
- 3 garlic cloves, minced
- 2 teaspoon cumin, ground
- 1 and 1/2 teaspoon oregano, dried
- 2 cups white rice, already cooked
- 1 cup corn
- 1 tomato chopped
- 7 ounces canned pinto beans, drained
- 1 chipotle pepper in adobo
- A pinch of salt and black pepper
- 5 colored bell peppers, tops and insides scooped out
- 1/2 cup vegan enchilada sauce

Directions:

1. Heat up a pan with the oil over medium high heat, add onion and celery, stir and cook for 5 minutes.
2. Add garlic, stir, cook for 1 minute more, take off heat and mix with chili, cumin and oregano.
3. Also add rice, corn, beans, tomato, salt, pepper and chipotle pepper and stir well.
4. Stuff bell peppers with this mix and place them in your slow cooker.
5. Add enchilada sauce, cover and cook on Low for 4 hours.
6. Arrange stuffed bell peppers on a platter and serve them as an appetizer.
7. Enjoy!

Nutritional Value (Amount per Serving):

- Calories: 221
- Fat: 5
- Carbs: 19
- Protein: 3

Black Eyed Peas Pate

Prep Time: 10 Minutes   Cook Time: 5 Hours   Serves: 5

Ingredients:

- 1 and 1/2 cups black-eyed peas
- 3 cups water
- 1 teaspoon Cajun seasoning
- 1/2 cup pecans, toasted
- 1/2 teaspoon garlic powder
- 1/2 teaspoon jalapeno powder
- A pinch of salt and black pepper
- 1/4 teaspoon liquid smoke
- 1/2 teaspoon Tabasco sauce

Directions:

1. In your slow cooker, mix black-eyed pea with Cajun seasoning, salt, pepper and water, stir, cover and cook on High for 5 hours.
2. Drain, transfer to a blender, add pecans, garlic powder, jalapeno powder, Tabasco sauce, liquid smoke, more salt and pepper, pulse well and serve as an appetizer.
3. Enjoy!

Nutritional Value (Amount per Serving):

- Calories: 221
- Fat: 4
- Carbs: 16
- Protein: 4

Tofu Appetizer

Prep Time: 10 Minutes   Cook Time: 7 Hours   Serves: 6

Ingredients:

- 1/4 cup yellow onions, sliced
- 1 cup carrot, sliced
- 14 ounces firm tofu, cubed

For the sauce:

- 1/4 cup soy sauce
- 1/2 cup water
- 3 tablespoons agave nectar
- 3 tablespoons nutritional yeast
- 1 tablespoon garlic, minced
- 1 tablespoon ginger, minced
- 1/2 tablespoon rice vinegar

Directions:

1. In your slow cooker, mix tofu with onion and carrots.
2. In a bowl, mix soy sauce with water, agave nectar, yeast, garlic, ginger and vinegar and whisk well.
3. Add this to slow cooker, cover and cook on Low for 7 hours.
4. Divide into appetizer bowls and serve.
5. Enjoy!

Nutritional Value (Amount per Serving):

- Calories: 251
- Fat: 6
- Carbs: 12
- Protein: 3

Artichoke Spread

Ingredients:

- 28 ounces canned artichokes, drained and chopped
- 10 ounces spinach
- 8 ounces coconut cream
- 1 yellow onion, chopped
- 2 garlic cloves, minced
- 3/4 cup coconut milk
- 1/2 cup tofu, pressed and crumbled
- 1/3 cup vegan avocado mayonnaise
- 1 tablespoon red vinegar
- A pinch of salt and black pepper

Directions:

1. In your slow cooker, mix artichokes with spinach, coconut cream, onion, garlic, coconut milk, tofu, avocado mayo, vinegar, salt and pepper, stir well, cover and cook on Low for 2 hours.
2. Divide into bowls and serve as an appetizer.
3. Enjoy!

Nutritional Value (Amount per Serving):

- Calories: 355
- Fat: 24
- Carbs: 19
- Protein: 13

Black Bean Appetizer Salad

Ingredients:

- 1 tablespoon coconut aminos
- 1/2 teaspoon cumin, ground
- 1 cup canned black beans
- 1 cup salsa
- 6 cups romaine lettuce leaves
- 1/2 cup avocado, peeled, pitted and mashed

Directions:

1. In your slow cooker, mix black beans with salsa, cumin and aminos, stir, cover and cook on Low for 4 hours.
2. In a salad bowl, mix lettuce leaves with black beans mix and mashed avocado, toss and serve as an appetizer.
3. Enjoy!

Nutritional Value (Amount per Serving):

- Calories: 221
- Fat: 4
- Carbs: 12
- Protein: 3

Three Bean Dip

Prep Time: 10 Minutes   Cook Time: 1 Hours   Serves: 6

Ingredients:

- 1/2 cup salsa
- 2 cups canned refried beans
- 1 cup vegan nacho cheese
- 2 tablespoons green onions, chopped

Directions:

1. In your slow cooker, mix refried beans with salsa, vegan nacho cheese and green onions, stir, cover and cook on High for 1 hour.
2. Divide into bowls and serve as a party snack.
3. Enjoy!

Nutritional Value (Amount per Serving):

- Calories: 262
- Fat: 5
- Carbs: 20
- Protein: 3

Great Bolognese Dip

Prep Time: 10 Minutes   Cook Time: 5 Hours   Serves: 7

Ingredients:

- 1/2 cauliflower head, riced in your blender
- 54 ounces canned tomatoes, crushed
- 10 ounces white mushrooms, chopped
- 2 cups carrots, shredded
- 2 cups eggplant, cubed
- 6 garlic cloves, minced
- 2 tablespoons agave nectar
- 2 tablespoons balsamic vinegar
- 2 tablespoons tomato paste
- 1 tablespoon basil, chopped
- 1 and 1/2 tablespoons oregano, chopped
- 1 and 1/2 teaspoons rosemary, dried
- A pinch of salt and black pepper

Directions:

1. In your slow cooker, mix cauliflower rice with tomatoes, mushrooms, carrots, eggplant cubes, garlic, agave nectar, balsamic vinegar, tomato paste, rosemary, salt and pepper, stir, cover and cook on High for 5 hours.
2. Add basil and oregano, stir again, divide into bowls and serve as a dip.
3. Enjoy!

Nutritional Value (Amount per Serving):

- Calories: 251
- Fat: 7
- Carbs: 10
- Protein: 6

Eggplant Appetizer

Prep Time: 10 Minutes   Cook Time: 7 Hours   Serves: 4

Ingredients:

- 1 and 1/2 cups tomatoes, chopped
- 3 cups eggplant, cubed
- 2 teaspoons capers
- 6 ounces green olives, pitted and sliced
- 4 garlic cloves, minced
- 2 teaspoons balsamic vinegar
- 1 tablespoon basil, chopped
- Salt and black pepper to the taste

Directions:

1. In your slow cooker, mix tomatoes with eggplant cubes, capers, green olives, garlic, vinegar, basil, salt and pepper, toss, cover and cook on Low for 7 hours.
2. Divide into small appetizer plates and serve as an appetizer.
3. Enjoy!

Nutritional Value (Amount per Serving):

- Calories: 200
- Fat: 6
- Carbs: 9
- Protein: 2

CHAPTER 6: SOUP AND STEW

Savory Lemony Lentil and Chicken Soup

Prep Time: 15 Minutes   Cook Time: 6 Hours   Serves: 6

Ingredients:

- 1 medium yellow onion, very thinly sliced
- 1 cup brown lentils
- 1 pound boneless, skinless chicken thighs, trimmed of excess fat
- 1 teaspoon garlic powder
- 5 cups chicken broth
- 3 large egg yolks
- ¼ cup fresh lemon juice
- Salt
- Freshly ground black pepper

Directions:

1. Combine the chicken, garlic powder, onion, lentils, and chicken broth in the slow cooker.
2. Cover with the lid and cook on low for 6 hours.
3. Remove the chicken to a cutting board. Shred the chicken with two forks and move it back to the slow cooker.
4. Whisk together the egg yolks and lemon juice in a small bowl. Stir the mixture into the slow cooker. Season with salt and pepper and serve bon appetite.

Nutritional Value (Amount per Serving):

- Calories: 277
- Fat: 8g
- Carb: 23g
- Protein: 29g

Savory Black Bean Soup

Prep Time: 10 Minutes   Cook Time: 8 Hours   Serves: 6

Ingredients:

- 8 ounces dried black beans, picked over and rinsed
- 3½ cups water
- 1 smoked ham hock, rinsed
- 1 bay leaf
- 1 teaspoon dried oregano
- 1 teaspoon ground cumin
- 1 teaspoon garlic powder
- 1 teaspoon salt, plus more for seasoning
- Juice of 1 lime
- 1 (8-ounce) can tomato sauce
- Freshly ground black pepper
- Chopped fresh cilantro, for garnish

Directions:

1. Combine the bay leaf, water, ham hock, black beans, cumin, oregano, garlic powder, and salt in the slow cooker.
2. Cover with the lid and cook on low for 8 hours, or until the beans are soft.
3. Discard the bay leaf. Blend in the lime juice and tomato sauce. Season with additional salt and pepper, if you like.
4. Ladle into soup bowls and garnish with cilantro, serve bon appetite.

Nutritional Value (Amount per Serving):

- Calories: 237
- Fat: 7g
- Carb: 23g
- Protein: 21g

Savory Beef and Barley Soup

Prep Time: 15 Minutes   Cook Time: 8 Hours   Serves: 6 To 8

Ingredients:

- 3 cups chicken broth
- 3 cups beef broth
- 1 tablespoon tomato paste
- 2 cups frozen mirepoix
- 1½ pounds beef chuck roast, trimmed of excess fat and cut into bite-size pieces
- ⅔ cup pearl barley (not quick-cooking)
- 8 ounces sliced mushrooms
- 1 bay leaf
- 1 teaspoon onion powder
- 1 teaspoon garlic powder
- ¾ teaspoon dried thyme
- 1 teaspoon salt, plus more for seasoning
- ½ teaspoon freshly ground black pepper, plus more for seasoning

Directions:

1. Combine all the ingredients in the slow cooker and mix.
2. Cover with the lid and cook on low for 8 hours.
3. Discard the bay leaf. Season with additional pepper and salt, if necessary. Ladle into bowls and serve bon appetite.

Nutritional Value (Amount per Serving):

- Calories: 298
- Fat: 9g
- Carb: 21g
- Protein: 31g

Savory Chicken Enchilada Soup

Prep Time: 10 Minutes   Cook Time: 8 Hours   Serves: 6

Ingredients:

- 1 cup chicken broth
- 1½ cups picante sauce
- 1 (15-ounce) can enchilada sauce
- 1 (14.5-ounce) can black beans, rinsed and drained
- 1½ pounds boneless, skinless chicken thighs, trimmed of excess fat
- 1 teaspoon ground cumin
- 1 (14.5-ounce) can refried beans
- Sour cream, for topping (optional)

Directions:

1. Combine the enchilada sauce, black beans, chicken, broth, picante sauce, and cumin in the slow cooker.
2. Cover with the lid and cook on low for 8 hours.
3. Remove the chicken to a cutting board. It should be very soft. Shred the chicken with two forks.
4. Put the refried beans to the slow cooker and mix until combined. Softly stir in the shredded chicken. Ladle the soup into bowls, top each serving with a dollop of sour cream (if you like), and serve bon appetite.

Nutritional Value (Amount per Serving):

- Calories: 273
- Fat: 8g
- Carb: 22g
- Protein: 28g

Tasty Chicken and Pesto Soup

Prep Time: 15 Minutes   Cook Time: 6 Hours   Serves: 6

Ingredients:

- 3½ cups chicken broth
- 2 carrots, peeled and cut into ¼-inch rounds
- 2 celery stalks, cut into ¼-inch slices
- 1 teaspoon dried oregano
- 1 teaspoon garlic powder
- 5 boneless, skinless chicken thighs, trimmed of excess fat
- ½ cup long-grain brown rice
- 1½ cups milk, at room temperature
- ½ cup basil pesto

Directions:

1. Combine the celery, oregano, broth, carrots, and garlic powder in the slow cooker and mix. Add the chicken and rice and mix.
2. Cover with the lid and cook on low for 6 hours, or until the chicken is cooked through and the rice is soft.
3. Remove the chicken to a cutting board. Shred the chicken with two forks or cut it into small pieces. Move the chicken back to the slow cooker. Stir in the milk and pesto.
4. Cover with the lid and cook on high for 10 minutes, until warmed through. Ladle into bowls and serve bon appetite.

Nutritional Value (Amount per Serving):

- Calories: 239
- Fat: 8g
- Carb: 18g
- Protein: 25g

Flavory Chicken and Barley Soup

Prep Time: 10 Minutes   Cook Time: 6 Hours   Serves: 6

Ingredients:

- 5 boneless, skinless chicken thighs, trimmed of excess fat
- ½ cup pearl barley (not quick-cooking)
- 3 cups frozen mirepoix
- 3½ cups chicken broth
- 1 (14.5-ounce) can diced tomatoes, undrained
- 1 tablespoon tomato paste
- 1 bay leaf
- 1 teaspoon dried basil
- 1 teaspoon garlic powder
- ¾ teaspoon salt, plus more for seasoning
- ¼ teaspoon freshly ground black pepper, plus more for seasoning

Directions:

1. Mix all the ingredients in the slow cooker and blend to combine.
2. Cover with the lid and cook on low for 6 hours.
3. Discard the bay leaf. Remove the chicken to a cutting board. Shred the chicken with two forks or cut it into small pieces. Move the chicken back to the slow cooker. Season with additional pepper and salt, if you like. Ladle the soup into bowls and serve bon appetite.

Nutritional Value (Amount per Serving):

- Calories: 164
- Fat: 6g
- Carb: 6g
- Protein: 22g

Delicious Tomato Soup

Prep Time: 10 Minutes   Cook Time: 8 Hours   Serves: 6

Ingredients:

- 1 cup frozen mirepoix
- ⅓ cup all-purpose flour
- 1 (28-ounce) can crushed tomatoes
- 1 (6-ounce) can tomato paste
- 1 tablespoon dried basil
- 1 teaspoon dried oregano
- 1 teaspoon salt, plus more for seasoning
- 4 cups chicken or vegetable broth
- 1 bay leaf
- 1 cup milk, warmed
- 2 tablespoons unsalted butter
- Freshly ground black pepper
- ⅔ cup grated Parmesan cheese

Directions:

1. Mix the flour, mirepoix, tomato paste, crushed tomatoes, basil, oregano, and salt in the slow cooker. Use a whisk to blend the flour into the tomatoes to incorporate. Add the broth and blend. Add the bay leaf.
2. Cover with the lid and cook on low for 8 hours.
3. Discard the bay leaf. Stir in the butter and warm milk until the butter is melted. Season with additional salt and pepper, if you like.
4. Ladle the soup into bowls, put Parmesan cheese on the top, and serve.

Nutritional Value (Amount per Serving):

- Calories: 200
- Fat: 8g
- Carb: 25g
- Protein: 11g

Delicious Creamy Cauliflower-Broccoli Soup

Prep Time: 10 Minutes   Cook Time: 8 Hours   Serves: 6

Ingredients:

- 2 pounds cauliflower florets
- 2 scallions, minced
- 2 cups chicken or vegetable broth
- 1 teaspoon onion powder
- 1 teaspoon garlic powder
- ¼ teaspoon dried thyme
- ½ teaspoon salt, plus more for seasoning
- ¼ teaspoon freshly ground black pepper, plus more for seasoning
- 1 (12-ounce) package frozen broccoli florets
- ½ cup grated Parmesan cheese, plus more for optional garnish
- ¼ cup heavy cream

Directions:

1. Combine the broth, onion powder, thyme, salt, cauliflower, scallions, garlic powder, and pepper in the slow cooker.
2. Cover with the lid and cook on low for 8 hours.
3. Carefully remove the contents of the slow cooker to a blender, in batches if needed. Purée until smooth, making sure to vent the blender lid for steam. Pour the puréed soup back into the slow cooker.
4. Blend in the Parmesan cheese, broccoli, and cream. Cover with the lid and cook on high for 10 minutes, or until heated through.
5. Season with additional pepper and salt, if necessary. Ladle the soup into bowls and garnish with more Parmesan cheese, if you like.

Nutritional Value (Amount per Serving):

- Calories: 124
- Fat: 5g
- Carb: 14g
- Protein: 10g

Flavor-packed Ham and White Bean Soup

Prep Time: 10 Minutes   Cook Time: 8 Hours   Serves: 8

(Plus Soaking The Beans Overnight)

Ingredients:

- 1 pound dried great northern beans, picked over and rinsed
- 1 tablespoon salt, plus ½ teaspoon, divided
- 6 cups chicken broth
- 6 cups water
- 2 cups cubed ham
- 2 cups frozen mirepoix
- 1 teaspoon dried basil
- 1 teaspoon dried oregano
- ¼ teaspoon freshly ground black pepper, plus more for seasoning
- 2 bay leaves
- ½ teaspoon liquid smoke

Directions:

1. The night before you make the soup, place the beans in a large bowl and add enough water to cover them by 2 inches. Spray in 1 tablespoon of salt. Soak the beans for more than 8 hours.
2. The next day, drain the water and rinse the beans completly. Place the beans in the slow cooker. Add the chicken broth, 6 cups fresh water, basil, oregano, ham, mirepoix, remaining ½ teaspoon of salt, pepper, bay leaves, water, and liquid smoke.
3. Cover with the lid and cook on low for 8 hours, or until the beans are soft.
4. Discard the bay leaves. Season with additional pepper and salt, if you like. Ladle into bowls and serve bon appetite.

Nutritional Value (Amount per Serving):

- Calories: 287
- Fat: 3g
- Carb: 42g
- Protein: 24g

Delicious French Onion Soup

Prep Time: 15 Minutes   Cook Time: 8 Hours   Serves: 4

Ingredients:

- 3 small yellow onions, cut into thin rings
- ¼ cup olive oil or canola oil
- Pinch salt
- Pinch freshly ground black pepper
- Pinch sugar
- 2 (13.5-ounce) cans beef consommé
- ½ cup water
- 4 slices crusty bread (French bread or a baguette works well)
- 1 ⅓ cups shredded Gruyère cheese

Directions:

1. Place the onions in the slow cooker. Add the salt, pepper, olive oil, and sugar and stir until the onions are well coated.
2. Cover with the lid and cook on low for 8 hours, or until the onions are tender and caramelized.
3. Put in the consommé and water and turn the slow cooker to high. Cook until heated through, about 10 minutes.
4. Position the top oven rack about 6 inches below the broiler. Switch on the broiler.
5. Ladle the soup into four oven-safe bowls and put them on a rimmed baking sheet. Put a piece of bread on the top of each serving of soup. Spray ⅓ cup of Gruyère cheese on the top of each piece of bread.
6. Broil for about 1 to 2 minutes, or until the cheese is melted and starts to brown. Serve right away.

Nutritional Value (Amount per Serving):

- Calories: 384
- Fat: 24g
- Carb: 28g
- Protein: 17g

CHAPTER 7: MEAT

Healthy Lentil and Bean Salad

Ingredients:

- 1 cup vegetable broth
- 1 (15-ounce) can pinto beans, rinsed and drained
- ⅔ cup brown lentils
- 3 tablespoons fresh lime juice, divided
- 1 teaspoon garlic powder
- ¼ teaspoon dried oregano
- ½ teaspoon salt, plus more for seasoning
- 6 ounces cherry tomatoes, halved
- 2 teaspoons olive oil
- 1 ounce queso fresco, crumbled
- Freshly ground black pepper

Directions:

1. Combine the beans, vegetable broth, lentils, garlic powder, oregano, 1 tablespoon of lime juice, and salt in the slow cooker.
2. Cover with the lid and cook on low for 4 hours.
3. Stir in the remaining 2 tablespoons of lime juice, olive oil, cherry tomatoes, and queso fresco. Season with additional pepper and salt, if you like, and serve.

Nutritional Value (Amount per Serving):

- Calories: 613
- Fat: 12g
- Carb: 100g
- Protein: 39g

Tasty Ratatouille

Prep Time: 15 Minutes   Cook Time: 5 Hours   Serves: 4

Ingredients:

- 1 medium yellow onion, diced
- 2 tablespoons olive oil, divided
- 1 tablespoon tomato paste
- 2 teaspoons garlic powder
- 1 teaspoon dried basil
- ¼ teaspoon salt, plus more for seasoning
- 8 ounces eggplant, cut into 1-inch dice
- 8 ounces zucchini, cut into 1-inch dice
- 1 large red, yellow, or orange bell pepper, seeded and cut into 1-inch pieces
- Freshly ground black pepper

Directions:

1. Mix the onion and 1 tablespoon of olive oil in a microwave-safe bowl. Cover with the lid and microwave on high for about 5 minutes, stirring halfway through. Stir in the tomato paste, salt, garlic powder, basil, and the remaining 1 tablespoon of olive oil. Pour the mixture into the slow cooker. Add the zucchini, eggplant, and bell pepper and mix.
2. Cover with the lid and cook on low for 5 hours.
3. Season with additional salt and pepper, if you like, and serve bon appetite.

Nutritional Value (Amount per Serving):

- Calories: 135
- Fat: 8g
- Carb: 17g
- Protein: 4g

Authentic Mexican Beans and Rice

Prep Time: 5 Minutes   Cook Time: 3 Hours   Serves: 4

Ingredients:

- 1 (15-ounce) can black beans, rinsed and drained
- ¾ cup long-grain brown rice
- 1½ cups water
- ¾ cup salsa or picante sauce, plus more if desired
- 1 bay leaf
- 1 teaspoon ground cumin
- ½ teaspoon garlic powder
- ½ teaspoon salt
- 1 to 2 tablespoons fresh lime juice
- Sour cream, for topping (optional)

Directions:

1. Combine the salsa, bay leaf, cumin, garlic powder, beans, rice, water, and salt in the slow cooker.
2. Cover with the lid and cook on low for 3 hours.
3. Discard the bay leaf. Put the lime juice and additional salsa, if you like.
4. Serve with a dollop of sour cream (if necessary).

Nutritional Value (Amount per Serving):

- Calories: 262
- Fat: 2g
- Carb: 52g
- Protein: 11g

Tasty Spaghetti Squash with Feta

Prep Time: 5 Minutes   Cook Time: 6 Hours   Serves: 2

Ingredients:

- 1 small (1- to 2-pound) spaghetti squash
- 1 cup water
- ¼ cup heavy cream
- 3 garlic cloves, minced
- 3 tablespoons unsalted butter
- ½ cup feta cheese
- Salt
- Freshly ground black pepper
- 2 tablespoons chopped fresh parsley, for garnish

Directions:

1. Make 6 to 8 slits all over the spaghetti squash with a sharp knife. Place the squash in the slow cooker. Add the water.
2. Cover with the lid and cook on low for 6 hours.
3. Remove the squash to a cutting board and allow it to cool slightly. Once you can handle it, cut the squash lengthwise and scoop out the seeds. Scrape the flesh to create long strands resembling spaghetti with a fork.
4. Move the squash strands back to the slow cooker and turn to low. Add the garlic, cream, and butter and stir softly to combine. Add the feta. Season with salt and pepper. Garnish with chopped parsley and serve bon appetite.

Nutritional Value (Amount per Serving):

- Calories: 453
- Fat: 34g
- Carb: 35g
- Protein: 9g

Savory Zucchini Noodles with Marinara Sauce

Prep Time: 15 Minutes   Cook Time: 8 Hours   Serves: 6

Ingredients:

- 2 (28-ounce) cans crushed tomatoes
- 1 (14.5-ounce) can diced tomatoes with green peppers and onion
- 1 (6-ounce) can tomato paste
- 1 bay leaf
- 2 teaspoons dried basil
- 1 teaspoon garlic powder
- ½ teaspoon dried oregano
- 1 teaspoon brown sugar
- 2 tablespoons olive oil
- Salt
- Freshly ground black pepper
- 4 medium zucchini, trimmed

Directions:

1. Combine the iced tomatoes, crushed tomatoes with their juice, tomato paste, garlic powder, oregano, bay leaf, basil, and brown sugar in the slow cooker. Stir to mix.
2. Cover with the lid and cook on low for 8 hours.
3. Discard the bay leaf. Stir in the olive oil. Season with pepper and salt.
4. Make zucchini noodles with a spiralizer. (If you don't have a spiralizer, use a potato peeler.) Put the zucchini noodles in a microwave-safe dish and microwave on high for 3 minutes. Pile the zucchini on individual serving plates and put marinara sauce on the top.

Nutritional Value (Amount per Serving):

- Calories: 156
- Fat: 5g
- Carb: 24g
- Protein: 7g

Healthy Coconut Curry with Vegetables

Prep Time: 5 Minutes   Cook Time: 4 Hours   Serves: 4

Ingredients:

- 1 (13.5-ounce) can coconut milk, stirred
- 2 tablespoons red curry paste
- 2 tablespoons instant tapioca
- 1 (1-pound) package frozen stir-fry vegetables
- 1 (15-ounce) can chickpeas, rinsed and drained
- Salt
- Freshly ground black pepper

Directions:

1. Combine the curry paste, coconut milk, and tapioca in the slow cooker. Stir until the curry paste is completely blended into the milk. Stir in the vegetables and chickpeas.
2. Cover with the lid and cook on low for 4 hours.
3. Season with pepper and salt and serve bon appetite.

Nutritional Value (Amount per Serving):

- Calories: 483
- Fat: 28g
- Carb: 50g
- Protein: 10g

Authentic Mexican Quinoa Bowl

Prep Time: 10 Minutes   Cook Time: 3 Hours   Serves: 4

Ingredients:

- 1 cup quinoa, rinsed and drained
- 1½ cups water
- 1 (10-ounce) can diced tomatoes with green chiles
- 1 (15-ounce) can black beans, rinsed and drained
- 2 tablespoons fresh lime juice
- 1 teaspoon garlic powder
- ½ teaspoon salt
- Freshly ground black pepper
- 1 avocado, peeled, pitted, and sliced

Directions:

1. Combine the diced tomatoes quinoa, water, with their juices, lime juice, black beans, garlic powder, and salt in the slow cooker.
2. Cover with and cook on low for 3 hours. Move away the lid and fluff the ingredients with a fork. Season with additional pepper and salt, if necessary.
3. Scoop the quinoa and vegetables into serving bowls. Put avocado slices on the top of each portion. Serve.

Nutritional Value (Amount per Serving):

- Calories: 395
- Fat: 13g
- Carb: 57g
- Protein: 61g

Delicious Baked Potatoes with Avocado Pico de Gallo

Prep Time: 5 Minutes   Cook Time: 8 Hours   Serves: 6

Ingredients:

- 6 russet potatoes
- 2 tablespoons olive oil
- ⅓ cup finely chopped red onion
- 4 Roma tomatoes, finely chopped
- ⅓ cup chopped fresh cilantro
- 1 ripe avocado, peeled, pitted, and finely chopped
- Salt
- Freshly ground black pepper

Directions:

1. Scrub the potatoes completely and dry with paper towels. Chop each with a fork in several places. Rub them with olive oil. Wrap each potato tightly in aluminum foil. Place the potatoes in the slow cooker.
2. Cover with the lid and cook on low for 8 hours, or until the potatoes are soft when pierced with a fork. Move the wrapped potatoes away from the slow cooker, cover with a towel to keep warm, and set aside.
3. To prepare the pico de gallo, gently stir together the tomatoes, cilantro, onion, and avocado in a medium bowl. Season with salt and pepper.
4. Unwrap each potato and halve lengthwise. Use a fork to fluff the potato flesh. Top each potato with a generous portion of pico de gallo and serve bon appetite.

Nutritional Value (Amount per Serving):

- Calories: 410
- Fat: 12g
- Carb: 72g
- Protein: 9g

CHAPTER 8: DESSERTS

Fruit Compote

Prep Time: 10 Minutes   Cook Time: 4 Hours   Serves: 6

Ingredients:

- 1-quart water
- 1 cup coconut sugar
- 1 pound mixed apples, pears and cranberries, dried
- 5-star anise
- 2 cinnamon sticks
- Zest from 1 orange, grated
- A pinch cloves, ground
- Zest from 1 lemon, grated

Directions:

1. Put the water and the sugar in your slow cooker and stir well.
2. Add dried fruits, star anise, cinnamon, orange and lemon zest and cloves.
3. Stir, cover and cook on High for 4 hours.
4. Serve your compote warm in small dessert cups.
5. Enjoy!

Nutritional Value (Amount per Serving):

- Calories: 110
- Fat: 0
- Carbs: 3
- Protein: 5

Peanut Butter Cake

Prep Time: 10 Minutes   Cook Time: 2 Hours And 30 Minutes   Serves: 6

Ingredients:

- 1 cup almond flour
- 1/2 cup coconut sugar
- 3/4 cup coconut sugar
- 3 tablespoons cocoa powder
- 1/4 cup cocoa powder
- 1 and 1/2 teaspoons baking powder
- 2 tablespoons vegan margarine, melted
- 1/2 cup soy milk
- 1 teaspoon vanilla extract
- 1/2 cup peanut butter
- 2 cups hot water
- Cooking spray

Directions:

1. In a bowl, mix flour with 1/2 cup sugar, baking powder and 3 tablespoons cocoa powder and stir well.
2. Add margarine, soy milk and vanilla and stir well.
3. Grease your slow cooker with cooking spray and pour the cake mix in it.
4. In another bowl, mix 1/4 cup cocoa powder with 3/4 cup sugar and stir.
5. In a second bowl, mix peanut butter with hot water and whisk really well.
6. Combine cocoa powder mix with peanut butter one and stir everything.
7. Pour this over your cake batter, cover and cook on High for 2 hours and 30 minutes.
8. Leave the cake to cool down a bit, slice and serve.
9. Enjoy!

Nutritional Value (Amount per Serving):

- Calories: 220
- Fat: 3
- Carbs: 6
- Protein: 10

Apple Crisp

Prep Time: 10 Minutes   Cook Time: 3 Hours   Serves: 6

Ingredients:

- 6 apples, cored, peeled and sliced
- 1 and 1/2 cups almond flour
- Cooking spray
- 1 cup palm sugar
- 1/2 teaspoon nutmeg, ground
- 1 tablespoon cinnamon powder
- 1/4 teaspoon ginger powder
- 3/4 cup coconut butter, melted

Directions:

1. Grease your slow cooker with cooking spray and arrange apple slices on it.
2. In a bowl, mix flour with palm sugar, ginger, cinnamon, nutmeg and coconut butter and stir using your hands.
3. Spread this mix over your apple slices, cover slow cooker and cook on High for 3 hours.
4. Divide into dessert bowls and serve.
5. Enjoy!

Nutritional Value (Amount per Serving):

- Calories: 160
- Fat: 5
- Carbs: 12
- Protein: 6

Strawberry Cobbler

Prep Time: 10 Minutes   Cook Time: 2 Hours   Serves: 4

Ingredients:

- 2 teaspoons baking powder
- 1 and 1/4 cups coconut sugar
- 2 and 1/2 cups almond flour
- 1/2 teaspoon cinnamon powder
- 2 tablespoons flax seed meal mixed with 1 tablespoon water
- 1/2 cup almond milk
- 4 tablespoons canola oil
- 6 cups strawberries, chopped
- 1/4 cup rolled oats
- 1/4 cup basil, chopped
- Cooking spray

Directions:

1. In a bowl, mix 2 cups flour with 1/4 cup sugar, baking powder, cinnamon, milk, oil and flax seed meal and stir really well.
2. In another bowl, mix the rest of the flour with the rest of the sugar, basil and strawberries and toss well.
3. Pour the batter into your slow cooker after you've sprayed with cooking spray and spread well.
4. Add strawberries mix on top, sprinkle rolled oats, cover and cook on High for 2 hours.
5. Leave cobbler to cool down a bit and serve.
6. Enjoy!

Nutritional Value (Amount per Serving):

- Calories: 130
- Fat: 4
- Carbs: 8
- Protein: 7

Spicy Pears

Prep Time: 10 Minutes   Cook Time: 4 Hours   Serves: 2

Ingredients:

- 2 cups orange juice
- 4 pears, peeled and cored
- 5 cardamom pods
- 1/4 cup maple syrup
- 1 cinnamon stick
- 1 small ginger piece, grated

Directions:

1. Place pears in your slow cooker.
2. Add cardamom, orange juice, maple syrup, cinnamon and ginger, cover and cook on Low for 4 hours.
3. Divide pears between plates and serve.
4. Enjoy!

Nutritional Value (Amount per Serving):

- Calories: 130
- Fat: 2
- Carbs: 6
- Protein: 4

Peach Cake

Prep Time: 10 Minutes   Cook Time: 2 Hours And 30 Minutes   Serves: 8

Ingredients:

- 10 tablespoons coconut butter, melted
- 45 ounces canned peaches, drained
- 1 and 2/3 cup palm sugar
- 1 teaspoon cinnamon powder
- 1/2 teaspoon nutmeg
- 1/2 teaspoon almond extract
- 2 teaspoons baking powder
- 2 tablespoons flaxseed meal mixed with 1 tablespoon water
- 2 cups almond flour
- 1 cup coconut milk

Directions:

1. Drizzle half of the butter on the bottom of your slow cooker.
2. In a bowl mix nutmeg with 2/3 cup sugar and cinnamon and stir well.
3. Spread this over the butter in your slow cooker.
4. Arrange peaches next and spread them evenly in the pot.
5. In a bowl, mix the rest of the butter with the rest of the sugar, coconut milk, almond extract and flaxseed meal and stir well.
6. In another bowl, mix flour with baking powder and stir.
7. Combine butter and sugar mix with the flour and stir well.
8. Pour this over the peaches, cover and cook on High for 2 hours and 3 0 minutes.
9. Leave the cake to cool down a bit and turn it upside down on a platter.
10. Serve cold.
11. Enjoy!

Nutritional Value (Amount per Serving):

- Calories: 200
- Fat: 4
- Carbs: 7
- Protein: 8

Pear Delight

Prep Time: 10 Minutes   Cook Time: 4 Hours   Serves: 12

Ingredients:

- 3 pears, cored, peeled and chopped
- 1/2 cup raisins
- 2 cups dried fruits, mixed
- 1/4 cup coconut sugar
- 1 tablespoon vinegar
- 1 teaspoon lemon zest, grated
- 1 teaspoon ginger powder
- A pinch of cinnamon powder

Directions:

1. Put the pears in your slow cooker.
2. Add raisins, fruits, sugar, vinegar, lemon zest, ginger powder and cinnamon, stir, cover and cook on Low for 4 hours.
3. Divide into small jars and serve whenever!
4. Enjoy!

Nutritional Value (Amount per Serving):

- Calories: 140
- Fat: 3
- Carbs: 6
- Protein: 6

Easy Almond Pudding

Prep Time: 10 Minutes   Cook Time: 2 Hours And 30 Minutes   Serves: 6

Ingredients:

- 1 mandarin, sliced
- Juice from 2 mandarins
- 2 tablespoons coconut sugar
- 4 ounces coconut butter, soft
- 2 tablespoons flax seed meal mixed with 1 tablespoon water
- 3/4 cup coconut sugar
- 3/4 cup almond flour
- 1 teaspoon baking powder
- 3/4 cup almonds, ground Cooking spray

Directions:

1. Grease a loaf pan cooking spray and sprinkle 2 tablespoons sugar on the bottom.
2. Arrange sliced Mandarin over the sugar and leave loaf pan aside for now.
3. In a bowl, mix butter with 3/4 cup sugar and flax seed meal mixed with water and stir really well.
4. Add almonds, flour, baking powder and the mandarin juice and stir again.
5. Spread this over mandarin slices, arrange pan in your slow cooker, cover and cook on High for 2 hours and 30 minutes.
6. Uncover, leave aside for a few minutes, transfer to a platter, slice and serve.
7. Enjoy!

Nutritional Value (Amount per Serving):

- Calories: 200
- Fat: 4
- Carbs: 5
- Protein: 6

Strawberry Jam

Prep Time: 10 Minutes   Cook Time: 3 Hours   Serves: 12

Ingredients:

- 2 tablespoons lemon juice
- 4 pints strawberries
- 4 cups coconut sugar

Directions:

1. Put strawberries in your slow cooker.
2. Add lemon juice and stir gently.
3. Add sugar, stir again, cover and cook on Low for 1 hour.
4. Stir and cook on Low for 1 more hour.
5. Stir again and cook for 1 last hour.
6. Divide into jars and serve whenever you like.
7. Enjoy!

Nutritional Value (Amount per Serving):

- Calories: 30
- Fat: 0
- Carbs: 6
- Protein: 1

Sweet Peanut Butter Cake

Prep Time: 10 Minutes   Cook Time: 2 Hours And 30 Minutes   Serves: 8

Ingredients:

- 1 cup coconut sugar
- 1 cup flour
- 3 tablespoons cocoa powder + 1/2 cup
- 1 and 1/2 teaspoons baking powder
- 1/2 cup almond milk
- 2 tablespoons coconut oil
- 2 cups hot water
- 1 teaspoon vanilla extract
- 1/2 cup peanut butter
- Cooking spray

Directions:

1. In a bowl, mix half of the coconut sugar with 3 tablespoons cocoa, flour and baking powder and stir well.
2. Add coconut oil, vanilla and milk, stir well and pour into your slow cooker greased with cooking spray.
3. In another bowl, mix the rest of the sugar with the rest of the cocoa, peanut butter and hot water, stir well and pour over the batter in the slow cooker.
4. Cover pot, cook on High for 2 hours and 30 minutes, slice cake and serve.
5. Enjoy!

Nutritional Value (Amount per Serving):

- Calories: 242
- Fat: 4
- Carbs: 8
- Protein: 4

CONCLUSION

Being busy does not give you the right to eat out at night. While eating out is convenient, you are not sure that the food that you are eating contains healthy ingredients. The thing is that you can eat delicious and healthy meals despite your busy schedule if you have a Crock Pot slow cooker.

With the Crock Pot slow cooker, you can prepare delicious meals any time of the day. With this Crock Pot Slow Cooker Cookbook 2022, you will impress everyone around you with your home cooked meals! Enjoy hassle-free cooking with your Crock Pot slow cooker.

happy cooking

APPENDIX RECIPE INDEX

CPSIA information can be obtained
at www.ICGtesting.com
Printed in the USA
LVHW022326090122
708166LV00005B/135

9 781803 801025